CREEPY CRA

D1649556

Contents

Alison Hawes

Story illustrated by
Frances Castle

Heinemann

Before Reading

Find out about

- Unusual pets like leaf insects, scorpions, praying mantids, tarantulas and iguanas

Tricky words

- people
- unusual
- insects
- difficult
- warm
- leaves

Introduce these tricky words and help the reader when they come across them later!

Text starter

Most people buy a cat or a dog as a pet, but some people buy more unusual pets. Some unusual pets are difficult to keep and some are difficult to feed.

Unusual Pets

Most people buy a cat or a dog as a pet.

But some people buy more unusual pets.

Can you see the leaf insect?

Leaf insects

Leaf insects are unusual pets. But they can be difficult to keep as they have to be kept warm.

Leaf insects look like leaves and they eat leaves too!

Scorpions

Scorpions are unusual pets.
A scorpion has to be fed on
live insects.

But look out!
Scorpions can sting!

Praying mantids

Praying mantids have to be kept warm in a tank. They have to be fed on live insects.

But praying mantids have to be kept on their own or they will eat each other!

Tarantulas

Tarantulas have to be kept on their own or they will eat each other.

But look out! Tarantulas can bite!

Green iguanas

Green iguanas are unusual pets. But they are very difficult to keep as they grow very big.

A baby green iguana is 25cm long. But it will grow to 200cm!

Green iguanas like to climb trees
– and people. But look out!
Iguanas have sharp claws!

Stick insects

Stick insects are unusual pets.
But they are not difficult to keep.

They do not bite or sting and
they just eat leaves!

Can you see the stick insect?

Text Detective

- Why do tarantulas have to be kept on their own?
- Which unusual pet would you like to have?

Word Detective

- **Phonic Focus:** Final consonant clusters
  Page 4: Sound out the four phonemes in 'kept'.
  Can you blend the two sounds at the end?
- Page 10: Think of three words to rhyme with 'sting'.
- Page 10: Find a word meaning 'hard'.

Super Speller

Read these words:

keep   kept   each

Now try to spell them!

HA! HA! HA!

Q Why was the centipede dropped from the football team?

A He took too long to put on his boots!

In this story

 Max

 Tom

 The shopkeeper

Tricky words

- tarantula
- laughed
- queue
- counter
- escaped
- hairy

Introduce these tricky words and help the reader when they come across them later!

Story starter

Max likes to play jokes on people. Each week he spends his pocket money at the joke shop. One day Max went shopping with his friend Tom. They went to the joke shop first, but Max didn't know what to buy.

Max
and the
Joke Tarantula

Max and Tom went shopping.

They went to the joke shop.

But Max didn't know what to buy.

Then Max saw a big joke tarantula.

"I will buy this!" laughed Max. "This will be the best joke *ever!*"

Tom had to buy food for his fish. So they went to the pet shop.

There were lots of people in the shop. But there was just one shopkeeper.
Tom was fed up.
"What a big queue!" he said.

Max said, "I know what to do!"
He put his joke tarantula on
the counter.

"Help!" he said. "My pet
tarantula has escaped!"

The people in the queue saw the tarantula's big hairy legs on the counter.

"Help! Help!" they said.

Would you be scared of a tarantula?

The people left their shopping and ran out of the shop. Max and Tom laughed and laughed.

But the shopkeeper didn't laugh. "I will get the tarantula for you," he said to Max.

"No! No! I will get it!" said Max. He didn't want the shopkeeper to see the tarantula was a toy.

"No. I will get it!" said the shopkeeper.

What do you think will happen next?

Max put out his hands.
"Here it is!" said the shopkeeper.

The shopkeeper put a big hairy
tarantula in Max's hands.

Max and Tom saw it was a *real* tarantula!

They ran out of the shop.

The shopkeeper laughed and laughed!

Quiz

Text Detective

- What did Max do to get rid of the queue?
- Do you think the shopkeeper played a good joke?

Word Detective

- **Phonic Focus:** Final consonant clusters
  Page 18: Sound out the four phonemes in 'help'.
  Can you blend the two sounds at the end?
- Page 22: Find two words which describe the tarantula.
- Page 23: Why is the word 'real' in bold print?

Super Speller

Read these words:

didn't   left   buy

Now try to spell them!

HA! HA! HA!

Q What do you get if you cross a tarantula with a rose?

A I don't know, but I wouldn't try to smell it!